Principles of Costing
Workbook

Aubrey Penning

Published by Osborne Books Limited
Tel 01905 748071
Email books@osbornebooks.co.uk
Website www.osbornebooks.co.uk

Design by Laura Ingham

Printed by CPI Group (UK) Limited, Croydon, CR0 4YY, on environmentally friendly, acid-free paper from managed forests.

British Library Cataloguing in Publication Data
A catalogue record for this book is available from the British Library

ISBN 978-1-911198-55-0

Contents

Introduction

Qualifications covered

This book has been written specifically to cover the Unit 'Principles of Costing' which is mandatory for the following qualifications:

AAT Level 2 Certificate in Accounting

AAT Certificate in Accounting – SCQF Level 6

This book contains Chapter Activities which provide extra practice material in addition to the activities included in the Osborne Books Tutorial text, and Practice Assessments to prepare the student for the computer based assessments. The latter are based directly on the structure, style and content of the sample assessment material provided by the AAT at www.aat.org.uk.

Suggested answers to the Chapter Activities and Practice Assessments are set out in this book.

Osborne Study and Revision Materials

Additional materials, tailored to the needs of students studying this unit and revising for the assessment, include:

- **Tutorials:** paperback books with practice activities
- **Wise Guides:** pocket-sized spiral bound revision cards
- **Student Zone:** access to Osborne Books online resources
- **Osborne Books App:** Osborne Books ebooks for mobiles and tablets

Visit www.osbornebooks.co.uk for details of study and revision resources and access to online material.

Chapter activities

1   The costing system

1.1   The table below lists some of the characteristics of financial accounting and management accounting systems. Indicate **two** characteristics for each system by putting a tick in the relevant column of the table below.

Characteristic	Financial Accounting	Management Accounting
Records transactions that have already happened		
Provides accounts that comply with legal requirements		
Looks in detail at future costs and income of products and services		
May use estimates where these are the most suitable form of information		

1.2   Hideaway Ltd is a manufacturer of garden sheds.

Classify the following costs into materials, labour or overheads by putting a tick in the relevant column of the table below.

Cost	Materials	Labour	Overheads
Wood used to make sheds			
Insurance of factory			
Wages of employees who cut window glass to size			
Wages of carpenter who assembles shed panels			

1.3   Hideaway Ltd is a manufacturer of garden sheds.

Classify the following costs by nature (direct or indirect) by putting a tick in the relevant column of the table below.

Cost	Direct	Indirect
Wood used to make sheds		
Insurance of factory		
Wages of employees who cut window glass to size		
Wages of carpenter who assembles shed panels		

1.4   Dave's Plaice is a takeaway fish and chip shop.

Classify the following costs by putting a tick in the column of the table below.

Cost	Direct Materials	Direct Labour	Indirect Costs
Potatoes used to make chips			
Maintenance of cooking equipment			
Wages of employees who fry fish and chips			
Gas to cook fish and chips			

1.5   Trendy Limited manufactures clothing.

Classify the costs by function (production, administration, or selling and distribution) by putting a tick in the relevant column of the table below.

Cost	Production	Administration	Selling and Distribution
Purchases of cloth			
Salespeople's salaries			
Insurance of office building			
Salaries of sewing machinists			

2 Cost centres and overhead absorption

2.1 Omega Ltd, a manufacturer of furniture, uses a numerical coding structure based on one profit centre and three cost centres as outlined below. Each code has a sub-code so each transaction will be coded as ***/***.

Profit/Cost Centre	Code	Sub-classification	Sub-code
Sales	100	UK Sales	500
		Overseas Sales	600
Production	200	Direct Cost	100
		Indirect Cost	200
Administration	300	Indirect Cost	200
Selling and Distribution	400	Indirect Cost	200

Code the following income and expense transactions, which have been extracted from purchase invoices, sales invoices and payroll, using the table below.

Transaction	Code
Factory lighting	
Warehouse repairs	
Sales to Newcastle, UK	
Sales to India	
Materials to upholster chairs	
Factory maintenance wages	

2.2 Smooth Running Limited operates a garage that repairs and maintains cars. It uses a coding system for its costs (materials, labour or overheads) and then further classifies each cost by nature (direct or indirect cost) as below. So, for example, the code for direct materials is A100.

Element of Cost	Code	Nature of Cost	Code
Materials	A	Direct	100
		Indirect	200
Labour	B	Direct	100
		Indirect	200
Overheads	C	Direct	100
		Indirect	200

Code the following costs, extracted from invoices and payroll, using the table below.

Transaction	Code
Wages of trainee mechanic	
Wages of receptionist	
Oil used for car servicing	
Depreciation of electronic tuning equipment used for car servicing	
Replacement parts used for car repairs	

2.3   Highstyle Limited is a company that owns two hairdressing salons. One salon is called Barberz, and the other is called Hats-off. Each salon is an investment centre.

The following is an extract from the coding manual used by the company.

Investment Centre	Code
Barberz Salon	B
Hats-off Salon	H
Revenue, Cost or Investment	**Code**
Salon sales revenue	100
Salon purchase of hair products	200
Labour costs	300
Overheads	400
Investment in shop assets	900

Each code consists of a letter followed by a 3 digit number.

Complete the following table with the appropriate codes.

Transaction	Code
Sales in Barberz Salon	
Purchase of new barber chair for Hats-off Salon	
Purchase of new wall mirrors for Barberz Salon	
Purchase of hair products for Barberz Salon	
Cost of rent at Barberz salon	
Cost of paying wages of Hats-off stylist	

2.4 A company has a single cost centre in its factory where several different products are made. The following budgeted data relates to the factory:

Overheads	£245,000
Total production (all products)	61,250
Direct labour hours	17,500
Machine hours	12,250

Product K is one of the products made in the factory. It has the following data per unit:

Direct materials cost	£16.00
Direct labour cost	£25.00
Direct labour hours	2 hours
Machine hours	1.5 hours

- Complete the following table to show the alternative overhead absorption rates and the total cost per unit of Product K using each absorption method.

- State which one of the three overhead absorption methods is **least** likely to be appropriate for this company, and why.

Overhead absorption method	Units of output £	Direct labour hours £	Machine hours £
Overhead absorption rate			
Product K costs (per unit):			
Direct materials			
Direct labour			
Overheads			
Total costs			

2.5   A company has a single cost centre in its factory where several different products are made. The following budgeted data relates to the factory:

Overheads	£486,900
Direct labour hours	57,500
Machine hours	35,850

Product M is one of the products made in the factory. It has the following data per unit:

Direct materials cost	£33.80
Direct labour cost at £11.00 per hour	£33.00
Machine hours	2.5 hours

Complete the following table to show the alternative overhead absorption rates and the total cost per unit of Product M using each absorption method. Round the overhead absorption rate to four decimal places of £, and calculate the overhead absorbed to the nearest penny.

Overhead absorption method	Direct labour hours £	Machine hours £
Overhead absorption rate		
Product M costs (per unit):		
Direct materials		
Direct labour		
Overheads		
Total costs		

2.6 Dai Limited is a manufacturing company with two cost centres in its factory; Assembly and Finishing. Both cost centres are labour intensive. The following data relates to the cost centres:

	Assembly	Finishing	Total
Budgeted indirect costs	£101,600	£56,800	£158,400
Budgeted direct labour hours	39,500	22,250	61,750

One of the products made in the factory is Product Z. Its manufacture takes 6 hours direct labour in Assembly, and 2 hours 30 minutes direct labour in Finishing.

Using the following tables, calculate the overhead absorption rates and the overheads that are absorbed into each unit of Product Z. Round all amounts to the nearest penny.

	Budgeted indirect costs £	Budgeted direct labour hours	Overhead absorption rate £
Assembly			
Finishing			

Product Z	Direct labour hours per unit	Overhead absorption rate £	Overhead absorbed £
Assembly			
Finishing			
Total			

3   Cost behaviour

3.1   Falcon Ltd is a manufacturer of toys.

Classify the following costs by their behaviour (fixed, variable, or semi-variable) by putting a tick in the relevant column of the table below.

Cost	Fixed	Variable	Semi-Variable
Managers' salaries			
Production workers paid a fixed wage plus a production-based bonus			
Packaging materials for finished toys			
Factory insurance			

3.2   Complete the table below showing stepped fixed costs, variable costs, total costs and unit cost at the different levels of production. Calculate unit cost to the nearest penny where appropriate. Stepped fixed costs increase to £25,000 when 3,000 or more units are produced.

Units	Stepped Fixed Costs	Variable Costs	Total Costs	Unit Cost
1,000	£20,000	£5,000	£25,000	£25.00
2,000	£	£	£	£
3,000	£	£	£	£
4,000	£	£	£	£

3.3   Omega Ltd is costing a single product which has the following cost details:

Variable Costs per unit

Materials	£5
Labour	£4
Total Fixed Overheads	£90,000

Complete the following total cost and unit cost table for a production level of 15,000 units.

	Total Cost	Unit Cost
Materials	£	£
Labour	£	£
Fixed Overheads	£	£
Total	£	£

3.4   Identify the type of cost behaviour (fixed, variable, or semi-variable) described in each statement by ticking the relevant boxes in the table below.

Statement	Fixed	Variable	Semi variable
At 4,000 units the cost is £10,000, and at 7,500 units the cost is £18,750			
At 2,500 units the cost is £20 per unit, and at 12,500 units the cost is £4 per unit			
At 1,200 units the cost is £4,100 and at 4,800 units the cost is £14,900			

3.5 A company that makes a single product has the following details about its costs.

- Stepped fixed costs are £60,000 per month for production below 5,000 units per month, and £84,000 for production at or above 5,000 units per month.
- Semi-variable costs contain a fixed element of £1,000, and a variable element of £3 per unit.
- Variable costs are £18 per unit.

Complete the following table to show monthly and unit costs for the production levels shown. Round unit costs to the nearest penny.

Monthly Production	Stepped Fixed Costs £	Semi-variable Costs £	Variable Costs £	Total Costs £	Unit Costs £
3,000					
5,000					
8,000					
10,000					

4   Inventory valuation and the manufacturing account

4.1   Identify the correct inventory (stock) valuation method from the characteristic given by putting a tick in the relevant column of the table below.

Characteristic	FIFO	LIFO	AVCO
Issues of inventory are valued at the oldest purchase cost			
Issues of inventory are valued at the average of the cost of purchases			
Inventory balance is valued at the most recent purchase cost			

4.2   Identify whether the following statements about inventory (stock) valuation are true or false by putting a tick in the relevant column of the table below.

	True	False
FIFO costs issues of inventory at the average purchase price		
AVCO costs issues of inventory at the oldest purchase price		
LIFO costs issues of inventory at the most recent purchase price		
LIFO values inventory balance at the most recent purchase price		
FIFO values inventory balance at the most recent purchase price		
AVCO values inventory balance at the latest purchase price		

4.3   Omega Ltd has the following movements in a certain type of inventory into and out of its stores for the month of March:

Date	Receipts		Issues	
	Units	**Cost**	**Units**	**Cost**
March 5	300	£900		£
March 8	200	£800		£
March 12	500	£2,200		£
March 18			600	£
March 25	400	£2,000		£

Complete the table below for the issue and closing inventory values

Method	Value of Issue on 18 March	Inventory at 31 March
FIFO	£	£
LIFO	£	£
AVCO	£	£

4.4   Magnum Ltd has the following movements in a certain type of inventory into and out of its stores for the month of September:

Date	Receipts		Issues	
	Units	**Cost**	**Units**	**Cost**
September 5	400	£800		£
September 8	250	£450		£
September 12			300	£
September 18	500	£1,200		£
September 25	400	£1,000		£

Complete the table below for the issue and closing inventory values.

Calculate final values to nearest £.

Method	Value of Issue on September 12	Inventory at 30 September
FIFO	£	£
LIFO	£	£
AVCO	£	£

4.5 Examine the following statements about inventory control policy. Analyse the statements into those that are true and those that are false, by placing a tick in the appropriate column.

Statement	True	False
Lead time is the time between an order being received by the supplier, and the goods leaving the supplier's stores		
The order quantity is the quantity of goods that should be ordered each time an order is placed		
Buffer stock is the extra quantity of inventory that is held in case things do not go according to plan		
The re-order level is the quantity of goods that should be ordered each time an order is placed		
Lead time is the time between an order being placed, and the goods arriving at the customer's premises		
When the inventory balance reaches the re-order level, an order should be placed for further supplies		

4.6   Place the following headings and amounts into the correct format of a manufacturing account on the right side of the table, making sure that the arithmetic of your account is accurate. The first entry has been made for you.

	£		£
Direct cost		Opening inventory of raw materials	10,000
Opening inventory of raw materials	10,000		
Closing inventory of work in progress	19,000		
Direct labour	30,000		
Opening inventory of work in progress	10,000		
Closing inventory of finished goods	14,000		
Closing inventory of raw materials	11,000		
Cost of goods sold			
Raw materials used	43,000		
Purchases of raw materials	44,000		
Cost of goods manufactured			
Opening inventory of finished goods	25,000		
Manufacturing overheads	21,000		
Manufacturing cost			

Calculate the following amounts:

- Direct cost
- Manufacturing cost
- Cost of goods manufactured
- Cost of goods sold

5 Labour costs

5.1 Identify the following statements as being true or false by putting a tick in the relevant column of the table below.

Payment Method	Time-rate	Piecework	Time-rate plus bonus
Labour is paid based entirely on the production level achieved			
Labour is paid according to hours worked, plus an extra amount if an agreed level of output is exceeded			
Labour is paid only according to hours worked			

5.2 Greville Ltd pays a time-rate of £12 per hour to its direct labour for a standard 38 hour week. Any of the labour force working in excess of 38 hours is paid an overtime rate of £18 per hour.

Calculate the gross wage for the week for the two workers in the table below.

Worker	Hours Worked	Basic Wage	Overtime Premium	Gross Wage
A Summer	38	£	£	£
S Cambridge	43	£	£	£

5.3 Omega Ltd uses a piecework method with a guaranteed minimum to pay labour in one of its factories. The rate used is £1.30 per unit produced. The minimum pay for a week is £420.

Calculate the gross wage for the week for the two workers in the table below.

Worker	Units Produced in Week	Gross Wage
V Singh	320	£
A Evans	390	£

5.4 Omega uses a time-rate method with bonus to pay its direct labour in one of its factories. The time-rate used is £10 per hour and a worker is expected to produce 20 units an hour. Anything over this and the worker is paid a bonus of £0.25 per unit.

Calculate the gross wage for the week including bonus for the three workers in the table below.

Worker	Hours Worked	Units Produced	Basic Wage	Bonus	Gross Wage
A Samuel	35	650	£	£	£
J McGovern	35	775	£	£	£
M Schaeffer	35	705	£	£	£

5.5 Identify the following statements as true or false by putting a tick in the relevant column of the table below.

	True	False
Indirect labour costs can be identified with the goods being made or the service being produced		
Total direct labour costs never alter when the level of activity changes		
The classification of labour costs into direct and indirect does not depend on the method of calculation of the pay		

6 Using budgets and calculation tools

6.1 Identify the following statements as being true or false by putting a tick in the relevant column of the table below.

	True	False
A budget is a financial plan for an organisation that is prepared in advance		
If actual costs are more than budgeted costs, the result is a favourable variance		

6.2 Greville Ltd has produced a performance report detailing budgeted and actual costs for last month.

Calculate the amount of the variance for each cost type (without + or – signs) and then determine whether it is adverse or favourable by putting a tick in the relevant column of the table below.

Cost Type	Budget £	Actual £	Variance £	Adverse	Favourable
Direct Materials	93,500	94,200			
Direct Labour	48,700	47,800			
Production Overheads	28,000	31,200			
Administration Overheads	28,900	27,700			
Selling and Distribution Overheads	23,800	23,100			

6.3   The following performance report for last month has been produced for Greville Ltd as summarised in the table below. Any variance in excess of 4% of budget is thought to be significant and should be reported to the relevant manager for review and appropriate action.

Examine the variances in the table below and indicate whether they are significant or not significant by putting a tick in the relevant column.

Cost Type	Budget £	Variance £	Adverse/ Favourable	Significant	Not Significant
Direct Materials	93,500	700	A		
Direct Labour	48,700	900	F		
Production Overheads	28,000	3,200	A		
Administration Overheads	28,900	1,200	F		
Selling and Distribution Overheads	23,800	700	F		

6.4   It was noted from the performance report for Greville Ltd for an earlier month that the following cost variances were significant:

•   Direct Materials Cost

•   Selling and Distribution Overheads

These variances needed to be reported to the relevant managers for review and appropriate action if required.

Select from the following list a relevant manager or managers for each significant variance to whom the performance report should be sent:

    HR Manager

    Production Manager

    Sales Manager

    Training manager

    Managing Director

    Distribution Manager

    Purchasing Manager

Variance	Manager
Direct Materials Cost	
Selling and Distribution Overheads	

6.5 Monitor Limited uses a spreadsheet to present budgeted and actual data, and calculate profit and variances. The following spreadsheet has been partly completed.

	A	B	C	D	E
1		Budget £	Actual £	Variance £	A / F
2	Income	450,000	446,000		
3	Materials	114,500	114,600		
4	Labour	123,100	119,000		
5	Overheads	170,500	174,100		
6	Profit				

Required:

- Enter A or F into each cell in column E to denote adverse or favourable variances.
- Enter appropriate formulas into the cells in column D to calculate variances, and into the remaining cells in row 6 to calculate profit.

6.6 Fairpay Limited has a section in which four employees work as a team. Each employee is paid a basic £16 for each hour worked. In addition, a team bonus is calculated each week and divided equally among the four employees. The total team bonus is £28 for each unit that the team produces in excess of 100 units.

During a specific week the employees had the following data.

Employee	Hours Worked	Units Produced
D. Kerr	39	
R. McGee	40	
S. Poole	38	
N. Carr	40	
Team output		112

The following spreadsheet (partly completed) is used to present the amount of pay for each member of the team.

	A	B	C	D	E	F
1		Team Production (units)	Minimum Production for bonus (units)	Excess Production (units)	Team bonus per excess unit £	Team Total Bonus £
2	Team Bonus Calculation		100		28	
3		D. Kerr	R. McGee	S. Poole	N. Carr	Team Total
4	Hours Worked					
5	Hourly Rate £	16	16	16	16	
6	Basic Pay £					
7	Bonus £					=F2
8	Total Pay £					

Row 2 is used to calculate the team bonus.

Rows 4 to 8 are used to calculate pay, with appropriate team totals shown in column F.

Required:

(a)   Complete the above spreadsheet as follows
- – enter the production data into B2, and suitable formulas into D2 and F2.
- – enter hours worked into row B4
- – enter appropriate formulas into the relevant remaining cells to provide the required information

(b)   In the separate spreadsheet extract below, show the figures to 2 decimal places that would appear in lines 6, 7, and 8, based on your formulas.

6	Basic Pay £				
7	Bonus £				
8	Total Pay £				

Answers to chapter activities

1 The costing system

1.1

Characteristic	Financial Accounting	Management Accounting
Records transactions that have already happened	✓	
Provides accounts that comply with legal requirements	✓	
Looks in detail at future costs and income of products and services		✓
May use estimates where these are the most suitable form of information		✓

1.2

Cost	Materials	Labour	Overheads
Wood used to make sheds	✓		
Insurance of factory			✓
Wages of employees who cut window glass to size		✓	
Wages of carpenter who assembles shed panels		✓	

1.3

Cost	Direct	Indirect
Wood used to make sheds	✓	
Insurance of factory		✓
Wages of employees who cut window glass to size	✓	
Wages of carpenter who assembles shed panels	✓	

1.4

Cost	Direct Materials	Direct Labour	Indirect Costs
Potatoes used to make chips	✓		
Maintenance of cooking equipment			✓
Wages of employees who fry fish and chips		✓	
Gas to cook fish and chips			✓

1.5

Cost	Production	Administration	Selling and Distribution
Purchases of cloth	✓		
Salespeople's salaries			✓
Insurance of office building		✓	
Salaries of sewing machinists	✓		

2 Cost centres and overhead absorption

2.1

Transaction	Code
Factory lighting	200/200
Warehouse repairs	400/200
Sales to Newcastle, UK	100/500
Sales to India	100/600
Materials to upholster chairs	200/100
Factory maintenance wages	200/200

2.2

Cost	Code
Wages of trainee mechanic	B100
Wages of receptionist	B200
Oil used for car servicing	A100
Depreciation of electronic tuning equipment used for car servicing	C200
Replacement parts used for car repairs	A100

2.3

Transaction	Code
Sales in Barberz Salon	B100
Purchase of new barber chair for Hats-off Salon	H900
Purchase of new wall mirrors for Barberz Salon	B900
Purchase of hair products for Barberz Salon	B200
Cost of rent at Barberz salon	B400
Cost of paying wages of Hats-off stylist	H300

2.4

Overhead absorption method	Units of output £	Direct labour hours £	Machine hours £
Overhead absorption rate	4.00	14.00	20.00
Product K costs (per unit):			
Direct materials	16.00	16.00	16.00
Direct labour	25.00	25.00	25.00
Overheads	4.00	28.00	30.00
Total costs	45.00	69.00	71.00

- The units of output method of overhead absorption is least likely to be appropriate since the company makes several different products, and under this system they would all be charged the same amount of overhead.

2.5

Overhead absorption method	Direct labour hours £	Machine hours £
Overhead absorption rate	8.4678	13.5816
Product M costs (per unit):		
Direct materials	33.80	33.80
Direct labour	33.00	33.00
Overheads	25.40	33.95
Total costs	92.20	100.75

2.6

	Budgeted indirect costs £	Budgeted direct labour hours	Overhead absorption rate £
Assembly	101,600	39,500	2.57
Finishing	56,800	22,250	2.55

Product Z	Direct labour hours per unit	Overhead absorption rate £	Overhead absorbed £
Assembly	6.0	2.57	15.42
Finishing	2.5	2.55	6.38
Total			21.80

3   Cost behaviour

3.1

Cost	Fixed	Variable	Semi-Variable
Managers' salaries	✓		
Production workers paid a fixed wage plus a production-based bonus			✓
Packaging materials for finished toys		✓	
Factory insurance	✓		

3.2

Units	Stepped Fixed Costs	Variable Costs	Total Costs	Unit Cost
1,000	£20,000	£5,000	£25,000	£25.00
2,000	£20,000	£10,000	£30,000	£15.00
3,000	£25,000	£15,000	£40,000	£13.33
4,000	£25,000	£20,000	£45,000	£11.25

3.3

	Total Cost	Unit Cost
Materials	£75,000	£5.00
Labour	£60,000	£4.00
Fixed Overheads	£90,000	£6.00
Total	£225,000	£15.00

3.4

Statement	Fixed	Variable	Semi-Variable
At 4,000 units the cost is £10,000, and at 7,500 units the cost is £18,750		✓	
At 2,500 units the cost is £20 per unit, and at 12,500 units the cost is £4 per unit	✓		
At 1,200 units the cost is £4,100 and at 4,800 units the cost is £14,900			✓

3.5

Monthly Production	Monthly Stepped Fixed Costs £	Monthly Semi-variable Costs £	Monthly Variable Costs £	Monthly Total Costs £	Unit Costs £
3,000	60,000	10,000	54,000	124,000	41.33
5,000	84,000	16,000	90,000	190,000	38.00
8,000	84,000	25,000	144,000	253,000	31.63
10,000	84,000	31,000	180,000	295,000	29.50

4 Inventory valuation and the manufacturing account

4.1

Characteristic	FIFO	LIFO	AVCO
Issues of inventory are valued at the oldest purchase cost	✓		
Issues of inventory are valued at the average of the cost of purchases			✓
Inventory balance is valued at the most recent purchase cost	✓		

4.2

	True	False
FIFO costs issues of inventory at the average purchase price		✓
AVCO costs issues of inventory at the oldest purchase price		✓
LIFO costs issues of inventory at the most recent purchase price	✓	
LIFO values inventory balance at the most recent purchase price		✓
FIFO values inventory balance at the most recent purchase price	✓	
AVCO values inventory balance at the latest purchase price		✓

4.3

Method	Value of Issue on 18 March	Inventory at 31 March
FIFO	£2,140	£3,760
LIFO	£2,600	£3,300
AVCO	£2,340	£3,560

4.4

Method	Value of Issue on September 12	Inventory at 30 September
FIFO	£600	£2,850
LIFO	£550	£2,900
AVCO	£577	£2,873

4.5

Statement	True	False
Lead time is the time between an order being received by the supplier, and the goods leaving the supplier's stores		✓
The order quantity is the quantity of goods that should be ordered each time an order is placed	✓	
Buffer stock is the extra quantity of inventory that is held in case things do not go according to plan	✓	
The re-order level is the quantity of goods that should be ordered each time an order is placed		✓
Lead time is the time between an order being placed, and the goods arriving at the customer's premises	✓	
When the inventory balance reaches the re-order level, an order should be placed for further supplies	✓	

4.6

	£		£
Direct cost		Opening inventory of raw materials	10,000
Opening inventory of raw materials	10,000	Purchases of raw materials	44,000
Closing inventory of work in progress	19,000	Closing inventory of raw materials	11,000
Direct labour	30,000	Raw materials used	43,000
Opening inventory of work in progress	10,000	Direct labour	30,000
Closing inventory of finished goods	14,000	**Direct cost**	
Closing inventory of raw materials	11,000	Manufacturing overheads	21,000
Cost of goods sold		**Manufacturing cost**	
Raw materials used	43,000	Opening inventory of work in progress	10,000
Purchases of raw materials	44,000	Closing inventory of work in progress	19,000
Cost of goods manufactured		**Cost of goods manufactured**	
Opening inventory of finished goods	25,000	Opening inventory of finished goods	25,000
Manufacturing overheads	21,000	Closing inventory of finished goods	14,000
Manufacturing cost		**Cost of goods sold**	

- Direct cost   £73,000
- Manufacturing cost   £94,000
- Cost of goods manufactured   £85,000
- Cost of goods sold   £96,000

5 Labour costs

5.1

Payment Method	Time-rate	Piecework	Time-rate plus bonus
Labour is paid based entirely on the production level achieved		✓	
Labour is paid according to hours worked, plus an extra amount if an agreed level of output is exceeded			✓
Labour is paid only according to hours worked	✓		

5.2

Worker	Hours Worked	Basic Wage	Overtime Premium	Gross Wage
A Summer	38	£456	£0	£456
S Cambridge	43	£516	£30	£546

5.3

Worker	Units Produced in Week	Gross Wage
V Singh	320	£420.00
A Evans	390	£507.00

5.4

Worker	Hours Worked	Units Produced	Basic Wage	Bonus	Gross Wage
A Samuel	35	650	£350.00	£0.00	£350.00
J McGovern	35	775	£350.00	£18.75	£368.75
M Schaeffer	35	705	£350.00	£1.25	£351.25

5.5

	True	False
Indirect labour costs can be identified with the goods being made or the service being produced		✓
Total direct labour costs never alter when the level of activity changes		✓
The classification of labour costs into direct and indirect does not depend on the method of calculation of the pay	✓	

6 Using budgets and calculation tools

6.1

	True	False
A budget is a financial plan for an organisation that is prepared in advance	✓	
If actual costs are more than budgeted costs the result is a favourable variance		✓

6.2

Cost Type	Budget £	Actual £	Variance £	Adverse	Favourable
Direct Materials	93,500	94,200	700	✓	
Direct Labour	48,700	47,800	900		✓
Production Overheads	28,000	31,200	3,200	✓	
Administration Overheads	28,900	27,700	1,200		✓
Selling and Distribution Overheads	23,800	23,100	700		✓

6.3

Cost Type	Budget £	Variance	Adverse/ Favourable	Significant	Not Significant
Direct Materials	93,500	£700	A		✓
Direct Labour	48,700	£900	F		✓
Production Overheads	28,000	£3,200	A	✓	
Administration Overheads	28,900	£1,200	F	✓	
Selling and Distribution Overheads	23,800	£700	F		✓

6.4

Variance	Manager
Direct Materials Cost	Production Manager or Purchasing Manager
Selling and Distribution Overheads	Sales Manager or Distribution Manager

6.5

	A	B	C	D	E
1		Budget £	Actual £	Variance £	A / F
2	Income	450,000	446,000	=C2-B2	A
3	Materials	114,500	114,600	=B3-C3	A
4	Labour	123,100	119,000	=B4-C4	F
5	Overheads	170,500	174,100	=B5-C5	A
6	Profit	=B2-B3-B4-B5	=C2-C3-C4-C5	=C6-B6	A

Other valid formulas could be used – for example, the formula in cell B6 could be =B2-SUM(B3:B5).

6.6 **(a)**

	A	B	C	D	E	F
1		Team Production (units)	Minimum Production for bonus (units)	Excess Production (units)	Team bonus per excess unit £	Team Total Bonus £
2	Team Bonus Calculation	112	100	=B2-C2	28	=D2*E2
3		D. Kerr	R. McGee	S. Poole	N. Carr	Team Total
4	Hours Worked	39	40	38	40	
5	Hourly Rate £	16	16	16	16	
6	Basic Pay £	=B4*B5	=C4*C5	=D4*D5	=E4*E5	=SUM(B6:E6)
7	Bonus £	=F7/4	=F7/4	=F7/4	=F7/4	=F2
8	Total Pay £	=B6+B7	=C6+C7	=D6+D7	=E6+E7	=SUM(B8:E8)

Note that in some cases, other formulas could be used to achieve the same results.

(b)

6	Basic Pay £	624.00	640.00	608.00	640.00	2,512.00
7	Bonus £	84.00	84.00	84.00	84.00	336.00
8	Total Pay £	708.00	724.00	692.00	724.00	2,848.00

Practice
Assessment 1

There may be parts of some tasks in this practice assessment that require the formatting of spreadsheet cells. Clearly this cannot be carried out in a paper-based practice assessment. The tasks are included to represent what you may be asked to carry out in a computer-based assessment, and the answers are presented to replicate the results of the required formatting.

Task 1

(a) **(1)** Identify **two** examples of terms used to classify cost **by function** from the following list.

Term	
Materials	
Fixed	
Administration	
Indirect	
Production	

(2) Complete the following sentences by using terms from the options:

(i) Costs that remain unchanged per unit of output are **fixed / variable / semi-variable** costs.

(ii) Costs that remain unchanged in total are **fixed / variable / semi-variable** costs.

(b) The table below lists some of the characteristics of financial accounting and management accounting systems.

Indicate which characteristics relate to each system by putting a tick in the relevant column of the table.

Characteristic	Financial Accounting	Management Accounting
It is concerned with recording historic costs and revenues		
One of its main purposes is to provide information for annual financial statements		
It is accurate, with no use of estimates		
It looks forward to show what is likely to happen in the future		

Task 2

Bromyard Ltd is looking to calculate the unit cost of one of the products it makes. It needs to calculate an overhead absorption rate to apply to each unit. The methods it is considering are:

•   Per machine hour

•   Per labour hour

•   Per unit

Total factory activity is forecast as follows:

Machine hours	35,000
Labour hours	60,000
Units	80,000
Overheads	£450,000

(a)   Complete the table below to show the possible overhead absorption rates that Bromyard Ltd could use. The absorption rates should be calculated to two decimal places.

	Machine hour	**Labour hour**	**Unit**
Overheads £			
Activity			
Absorption rate £			

The following data relates to the making of one unit of the product:

Material	5 kilos at £6 per kilo
Labour	30 minutes at £18 per hour
Production time	20 minutes machine time

(b)   Complete the table below (to two decimal places) to calculate the total unit cost, using the three overhead absorption rates you have calculated in (a).

Cost	Machine hour £	Labour hour £	Unit £
Material			
Labour			
Direct cost			
Overheads			
Total unit cost			

Task 3

(a)   Octavia Ltd, a manufacturer of food products, uses an alpha-numeric coding structure based on one profit centre and three cost centres as outlined below. Each code has a sub-code so each transaction will be coded as */***.

Profit/Cost Centre	Code	Sub-classification	Sub-code
Sales	A	Restaurant Sales	500
		Supermarket Sales	900
Production	B	Direct Cost	100
		Indirect Cost	200
Administration	C	Direct Cost	100
		Indirect Cost	200
Selling and Distribution	D	Direct Cost	100
		Indirect Cost	200

Code the following revenue and expense transactions, which have been extracted from purchase invoices, sales invoices and payroll, using the table below.

Transaction	Code
Factory lighting	
Repairs to warehouse	
Meat for making burgers	
Sales to 'Kings Restaurant'	
Commission to sales staff	
Stationery for Administration	

(b)   Complete the following sentences by using terms from the options:

(1)   An individual shop within a chain of shops that is responsible for capital expenditure would be an example of **a cost / an investment / a profit centre.**

(2)   A part of a business may be considered as a profit centre if it has responsibility for **income and costs / just costs / income, costs and investment.**

Task 4

(a)   Identify the type of cost behaviour (fixed, variable, or semi-variable) described in each statement by ticking the relevant boxes in the table below.

Costs	Fixed	Variable	Semi-variable
At 2,000 units the cost is £6,000, and at 9,000 units the cost is £27,000			
At 1,500 units the cost is £2,500, and at 3,500 units the cost is £4,500			
At 1,200 units the cost is £6,000, and at 2,000 units the cost is £3 per unit			

(b)   Complete the table below by inserting all costs for all activity levels.

	2,000 units	3,000 units	5,000 units	6,500 units
Variable cost £				13,000
Fixed cost £				
Total cost £		7,800	11,800	14,800

Task 5

A company has the following cost information for the last period:

	£
Purchases of raw materials	48,000
Direct labour	86,000
Indirect labour	14,000
Manufacturing expenses	50,000

Inventory information at the start and end of the period was as follows:

	£
Opening raw materials inventory	9,000
Closing raw materials inventory	10,000
Opening work in progress	9,000
Closing work in progress	11,000
Opening finished goods inventory	30,000
Closing finished goods inventory	25,000

Enter the correct figures for the following costs:

Format the Direct Materials Used and the Direct Cost as italics.

Format the remaining figures as bold.

Direct materials used £ _____

Direct cost £ _____

Manufacturing cost £ _____

Cost of goods manufactured £ _____

Cost of sales £ _____

Task 6

(a) Octavia Ltd has the following movements in a certain type of inventory (stock) into and out of its stores for the month of August:

Date	Receipts		Issues	
	Units	**Cost**	**Units**	**Cost**
August 12	100	£500		£
August 14	350	£1,820		£
August 17	400	£2,200		£
August 18			700	£
August 26	300	£1,680		£

Complete the table below for the issue and closing inventory values. Do not round values per unit in your calculation, but round final answers to the nearest £.

Method	Value of Issue on 18 August	Inventory at 31 August
FIFO	£	£
LIFO	£	£
AVCO	£	£

(b) Octavia Ltd uses a time-rate method with bonus to pay its direct labour in one of its factories. The time-rate used is £10 per hour and a worker is expected to produce 7 units an hour. Anything over this and the worker is paid a bonus of £0.50 per unit.

Calculate the gross wage for the week including bonus for the three workers in the table below.

Worker	Hours Worked	Units Produced	Basic Wage	Bonus	Gross Wage
A Weaton	40	250	£	£	£
J Davis	40	295	£	£	£
M Laston	40	280	£	£	£

Task 7

(a) A company has produced the following partial cost and revenue information for a product in the first quarter of the year:

Sales revenue per unit: £20

Variable costs per unit:

    Materials   £7

    Labour   £3

A spreadsheet has been partly completed to record the total costs and revenue.

	A	B	C	D	E	F	G
1	Month	Variable Materials £	Variable Labour £	Fixed Costs £		Sales Revenue £	
2	January	70,000	30,000	40,000	140,000	200,000	60,000
3	February	140,000					
4	March		45,000	40,000			
5	Total						

required:

- Insert appropriate column headings into cells E1 and G1 (select from: Total Variable Costs £; Total Fixed Costs £; Total Costs £; Profit £).
- Insert appropriate figures into the remaining cells in rows 3 and 4.
- Insert appropriate formulas into the cells in row 5.

(b) A company uses a spreadsheet to present budgeted and actual data and calculate profit and variances. The following spreadsheet has been partly completed.

	A	B	C	D	E
1		Budget £	Actual £	Variance £	A / F
2	Income	290,000	296,000		
3	Materials	144,500	150,600		
4	Labour	51,100	49,000		
5	Overheads	72,500	76,300		
6	Profit				

required:

- Enter A or F into each cell in column E to denote adverse or favourable variances.
- Enter appropriate formulas into the cells in column D to calculate variances and into the remaining cells in row 6 to calculate profit.
- Embolden the contents of row 1 and column E.

Practice
Assessment 2

There may be parts of some tasks in this practice assessment that require the formatting of spreadsheet cells. Clearly this cannot be carried out in a paper-based practice assessment. The tasks are included to represent what you may be asked to carry out in a computer-based assessment, and the answers are presented to replicate the results of the required formatting.

Task 1

(a) Indicate the characteristics of financial accounting and management accounting by putting a tick in the relevant column of the table below.

Characteristic	Financial Accounting	Management Accounting
The system is subject to many external regulations		
The accounts must be produced in a format that is imposed on the organisation		
The system is governed primarily by its usefulness to its internal users		
The information produced can be in any format that the organisation wishes to use		

(b) Olsen Ltd is a manufacturer of garden furniture.

Classify the following costs into material, labour or overheads by putting a tick in the relevant column of the table below.

Cost	Materials	Labour	Overheads
Wood used in garden chairs			
Rent of factory			
Wages of carpenters in the joinery section			
Expenses of the office manager			

Task 2

Ledbury Ltd is looking to calculate the unit cost of one of the products it makes. It needs to calculate an overhead absorption rate to apply to each unit. The methods it is considering are:

•   Per machine hour

•   Per labour hour

•   Per unit

Total factory activity is forecast as follows:

Machine hours	20,000
Labour hours	35,000
Units	75,000
Overheads	£380,000

(a)   Complete the table below to show the possible overhead absorption rates that Ledbury Ltd could use. The absorption rates should be calculated to two decimal places.

	Machine hour	**Labour hour**	**Unit**
Overheads £			
Activity			
Absorption rate £			

The following data relates to the making of one unit of the product:

Material	4 kilos at £7.50 per kilo
Labour	15 minutes at £16 per hour
Production time	10 minutes machine time

(b) Complete the table below (to two decimal places) to calculate the total unit cost, using the three overhead absorption rates you have calculated in (a).

Cost	Machine hour £	Labour hour £	Unit £
Material			
Labour			
Direct cost			
Overheads			
Total unit cost			

(c) Complete the following sentences by using terms from the options:

(1) Where an organisation produces many different products with different values it **should / should not** use a per unit overhead absorption method.

(2) For a labour-intensive manufacturing organisation, the most appropriate overhead absorption method would be **direct labour hours / machine hours.**

Task 3

(a)   Spread Ltd manages projects in the UK and abroad. It uses an alpha numerical coding structure as outlined below. Each code has a sub-code, so each transaction will have a code format AB123.

Activity	Code	Sub-classification	Sub-code
Investment in projects	IP	UK projects	100
		Overseas projects	200
Project revenues	PR	UK projects	100
		Overseas projects	200
Project costs	PC	Material	030
		Labour	040
		Overheads	050

Code the following transactions by entering the appropriate code in the table.

Transaction	Code
Revenue from project in Saudi Arabia	
Cost of material used for project in Saudi Arabia	
Cost of hiring local labour for project in Saudi Arabia	
Investment in project in Saudi Arabia	
Revenue from UK project	
Cost of renting project offices	

(b)   Identify **two** examples of terms used to classify cost **by element** from the following list.

Term	
Materials	
Fixed	
Administration	
Indirect	
Labour	

Task 4

Complete the table below by inserting all costs for all activity levels.

Round unit costs to 2 decimal places.

	5,000 units	6,000 units	10,000 units	10,500 units
Variable cost £		21,000		
Fixed cost £				
Total cost £		22,500	36,500	
Unit cost £				

Task 5

Reorder the following descriptions and amounts into a manufacturing account format on the right side of the table below. Where amounts are not shown, calculate them, and present them as emboldened figures in the appropriate places.

	£		£
Closing inventory of raw materials	10,000		
Direct labour	86,000		
Opening inventory of raw materials	9,000		
Closing inventory of finished goods	25,000		
Direct cost			
Cost of goods manufactured	195,000		
Cost of goods sold			
Manufacturing cost	197,000		
Purchases of raw materials	48,000		
Opening inventory of work in progress	9,000		
Opening inventory of finished goods	30,000		
Manufacturing overheads	64,000		
Direct materials used	47,000		
Closing inventory of work in progress	11,000		

Task 6

(a)   A business has the following movements in a certain type of inventory into and out of its stores for the month of February:

Date	Receipts		Issues	
	Units	**Cost**	**Units**	**Cost**
February 5	100	£400		£
February 9	300	£1,260		£
February 13	600	£2,640		£
February 18			800	£
February 26	500	£2,150		£

Complete the table below for the issue and closing inventory values.

Method	Cost of Issue on 18 February	Value of Inventory at 28 February
FIFO	£	£
LIFO	£	£
AVCO	£	£

(b) All production workers in a factory are paid at a basic rate of £10 per hour. Those who work the evening shift are paid an unsocial hours premium of 10% of basic pay. They are also paid for any overtime at basic rate plus an overtime premium of 25%, but overtime does not also attract an unsocial hour premium. There were ten production workers on the evening shift last month.

The factory sets a target for output each month of 50,000 units for the evening shift. Where this is exceeded, a bonus of £800 is shared between the production workers for every additional 1,000 units. The actual evening shift output last month was 52,000 units.

Complete the following table to show the total labour costs for the evening shift last month.

	Hours	Cost £
Basic hours and pay	1,400	
Unsocial hours premium		
Overtime hours basic rate	200	
Overtime hours premium		
Bonus payment		
Total pay		

Task 7

The following partially completed spreadsheet shows data regarding the last month for a company.

	A	B	C	D	E	F
1	Budgeted sales units	13,000		Budgeted selling price per unit £	64	
2	Budgeted material kg	14,150		Budgeted material price per kg £	11	
3	Budgeted labour hours	14,130		Budgeted labour rate per hour £	19	
4	Budgeted overheads £	£189,500				
5						
6		Budget £	Actual £	Variance £	Adv / Fav	Variance %
7	Sales		824,000			
8	Material		149,960			
9	Labour		281,050			
10	Overheads		191,400			
11	Profit		201,590			

Required:

Complete the spreadsheet lines 7 to 11 as follows:

- Complete cells B7 to B11 with formulas to calculate the budget figures. Format the cells to show in whole £.
- Complete cells D7 to D11 with formulas to calculate variances. The formulas should result in positive answers for favourable variances, and negative answers for adverse variances. Format the cells to show in whole £.
- Complete cells E7 to E11 with A or F to denote adverse or favourable variance.
- Complete cells F7 to F11 with formulas to show the percentage that each variance represents of the budget. Format the cells to round to two decimal places.

Practice
Assessment 3

There may be parts of some tasks in this practice assessment that require the formatting of spreadsheet cells. Clearly this cannot be carried out in a paper-based practice assessment. The tasks are included to represent what you may be asked to carry out in a computer-based assessment, and the answers are presented to replicate the results of the required formatting.

Task 1

(a)   The table below lists some of the characteristics of financial accounting and management accounting systems.

Indicate which characteristics relate to each system by putting a tick in the relevant column of the table below.

Characteristic	Financial Accounting	Management Accounting
One of its main outputs is a summarised historical financial statement that is produced annually		
One of its main purposes is useful information about costs within the organisation		
It can involve making comparisons between actual costs and budgeted costs		
Its output is controlled by legislation and accounting standards		

(b)   Carlsen Ltd is a manufacturer of windows.

Classify the following costs into material, labour or overheads by putting a tick in the relevant column of the table below.

Cost	Materials	Labour	Overheads
Aluminium used for window frames			
Insurance of factory			
Glass used to make windows			
Pay of employee who cuts glass to size and fits it into frames			

Task 2

Bedford Ltd is looking to calculate the unit cost of one of the products it makes. It needs to calculate an overhead absorption rate to apply to each unit. The methods it is considering are:

- Per machine hour

- Per labour hour

- Per unit

Total factory activity is forecast as follows:

Machine hours	90,000
Labour hours	235,000
Units	255,000
Overheads	£1,200,000

(a) Complete the table below to show the possible overhead absorption rates that Bedford Ltd could use. The absorption rates should be calculated to two decimal places.

	Machine hour	Labour hour	Unit
Overheads £			
Activity			
Absorption rate £			

The following data relates to the making of one unit of the product:

Material	9 kilos at £37.50 per kilo
Labour	1 hour at £23 per hour
Production time	30 minutes machine time

(b) Complete the table below (to two decimal places) to calculate the total unit cost, using the three overhead absorption rates you have calculated in (a).

Cost	Machine hour £	Labour hour £	Unit £
Material			
Labour			
Direct cost			
Overheads			
Total unit cost			

Task 3

(a) Complete the following table to analyse the examples of various responsibility centres.

	Cost centre	Profit centre	Investment centre
An autonomous overseas division of a multi-national organisation			
An assembly section within a factory production department			
The electrical goods section within a department store			

(b) Zoom Ltd operates a garage business which comprises second hand car sales and vehicle servicing. It uses an alpha-numeric coding structure based on one profit centre and three cost centres as outlined below. Each code has a sub-code so each transaction will be coded as */***.

Profit/Cost Centre	Code	Sub-classification	Sub-code
Sales	W	Second Hand Car Sales	300
		Vehicle Servicing Sales	400
Second Hand Cars	X	Direct Cost	100
		Indirect Cost	200
Vehicle Servicing	Y	Direct Cost	100
		Indirect Cost	200
Administration	Z	Direct Cost	100
		Indirect Cost	200

Code the following revenue and cost transactions, which have been extracted from purchase invoices, sales invoices and payroll, using the table below.

Transaction	Code
Revenue from sale of Ford car to Mr Smith	
Cost of maintenance of electronic diagnostic equipment used for servicing vehicles	
Revenue from servicing vehicles during April	
Purchase cost of second hand cars at auction	
Cost of oil used to service vehicles	
Cost of wax used to polish cars ready for sale	

Task 4

Complete the table below by inserting all costs for all activity levels.

Round cost per unit to 2 decimal places.

	12,000 units	12,500 units	16,000 units	16,500 units
Variable cost £	216,000	225,000	288,000	297,000
Fixed cost £	63,400	63,400	63,400	63,400
Total cost £	279,400	288,400	351,400	360,400
Cost per unit £	23.28	23.07	21.96	21.84

Task 5

(a)   A company has the following cost information for the last period:

	£
Raw materials used in production	117,000
Indirect raw materials	13,000
Direct labour	176,000
Indirect labour	15,000
Manufacturing expenses	98,000

Inventory information at the start and end of the period was as follows:

	£
Opening work in progress	37,000
Closing work in progress	49,000
Opening finished goods inventory	55,000
Closing finished goods inventory	38,000

Enter the correct figures for the following costs:

Cost structure for last period	£
Prime cost	
Manufacturing overheads	
Total manufacturing cost	
Cost of goods manufactured	
Cost of goods sold	

(b) Complete the following sentences relating to spreadsheets by inserting word(s) from the list given below.

-------------------------------- involves automatically using additional lines within a cell so that longer text can be seen.

-------------------------------- involves joining two adjacent cells together.

-------------------------------- can be used to place thick lines around the outside of a selected cell or group of cells.

Emboldening

Merging

Filling with colour

Entering data

Borders

Using italics

Text wrapping

Task 6

A company uses last in first out cost (LIFO) to value the issues and inventory of raw materials. The following record shows the inventory movements for the raw material P45 in December.

(a) Complete the inventory record. Costs per kilogram (kg) should be completed in £ to four decimal places.

| Date | Receipts | | | Issues | | | Balance | |
	Qty (kg)	Cost per kg	Total cost £	Qty (kg)	Cost per kg	Total cost £	Qty (kg)	Total cost £
1 Dec							20,000	50,000
6 Dec	15,000	2.65	39,750					
9 Dec				20,000				

(b) Complete the following table to show the value of the issue on 9 December and the inventory balance if the alternative valuation methods shown had been used. Do not round values per kg in your calculations, but round the final total valuations to the nearest £.

Method	Valuation of Issue £	Closing inventory value £
FIFO		
AVCO		

(c) Nelson Ltd uses a time-rate method with bonus to pay its direct labour in one of its factories. The time-rate used is £11.00 per hour and a worker is expected to produce 4 units an hour. Anything over this and the worker is paid a bonus of £1.50 per unit.

Calculate the gross wage for the week including bonus for the three workers in the table below.

Worker	Hours Worked	Units Produced	Basic Wage	Bonus	Gross Wage
J Jarvis	40	150	£	£	£
S Poole	40	185	£	£	£
D Kerr	40	173	£	£	£

Task 7

The following partially completed spreadsheet shows data regarding October for a company.

	A	B	C	D	E	F
1	Budgeted sales units for month		10,500	Budgeted selling price per unit £		12
2	Budgeted material for month kg		15,600	Budgeted material price per kg £		1.50
3	Budgeted labour hours for month		1,060	Budgeted labour rate per hour £		18
4	Budgeted annual overheads £		720,000			
5						
6		Budget £	Actual £	Variance £	Adv / Fav	Variance %
7	Sales		120,500			
8	Material		25,000			
9	Labour		19,500			
10	Overheads		61,000			
11	Profit		15,000			

Required:

Complete the spreadsheet lines 7 to 11 as follows:

- Complete cells B7 to B11 with formulas to calculate the budget figures. Format the cells to show in whole £.
- Complete cells D7 to D11 with formulas to calculate variances. The formulas should result in positive answers for favourable variances, and negative answers for adverse variances. Format the cells to show in whole £.
- Complete cells E7 to E11 with A or F to denote adverse or favourable variance.
- Complete cells F7 to F11 with formulas to show the percentage that each variance represents of the budget. Format the cells to round to two decimal places.

Answers to practice assessment 1

Task 1

(a)   **(1)**

Term	
Materials	
Fixed	
Administration	✓
Indirect	
Production	✓

(2)   **(i)**   Costs that remain unchanged per unit of output are **variable** costs.

(ii)   Costs that remain unchanged in total are **fixed** costs.

(b)

Characteristic	Financial Accounting	Management Accounting
It is concerned with recording historic costs and revenues	✓	
One of its main purposes is to provide information for annual financial statements	✓	
It is accurate, with no use of estimates	✓	
It looks forward to show what is likely to happen in the future		✓

Task 2

(a)

	Machine hour	**Labour hour**	**Unit**
Overheads £	450,000	450,000	450,000
Activity	35,000	60,000	80,000
Absorption rate £	12.86	7.50	5.63

(b)

Cost	**Machine hour £**	**Labour hour £**	**Unit £**
Material	30.00	30.00	30.00
Labour	9.00	9.00	9.00
Direct cost	39.00	39.00	39.00
Overheads	4.29	3.75	5.63
Total unit cost	43.29	42.75	44.63

Task 3

(a)

Transaction	**Code**
Factory lighting	B/200
Repairs to warehouse	D/200
Meat for making burgers	B/100
Sales to 'Kings Restaurant'	A/500
Commission to sales staff	D/200
Stationery for Administration	C/200

(b)　**(1)**　An individual shop within a chain of shops that is responsible for capital expenditure would be an example of **an investment** centre.

(2)　A part of a business may be considered as a profit centre if it has responsibility for **income and costs.**

Task 4

(a)

Costs	Fixed	Variable	Semi-variable
At 2,000 units the cost is £6,000, and at 9,000 units the cost is £27,000		✓	
At 1,500 units the cost is £2,500, and at 3,500 units the cost is £4,500			✓
At 1,200 units the cost is £6,000, and at 2,000 units the cost is £3 per unit	✓		

(b)

	2,000 units	3,000 units	5,000 units	6,500 units
Variable cost £	4,000	6,000	10,000	13,000
Fixed cost £	1,800	1,800	1,800	1,800
Total cost £	5,800	7,800	11,800	14,800

Task 5

Direct materials used	£47,000
Direct cost	£133,000
Manufacturing cost	**£197,000**
Cost of goods manufactured	**£195,000**
Cost of sales	**£200,000**

Task 6

(a)

Method	Value of Issue on 18 August	Inventory at 31 August
FIFO	£3,695	£2,505
LIFO	£3,760	£2,440
AVCO	£3,722	£2,478

(b)

Worker	Hours Worked	Units Produced	Basic Wage	Bonus	Gross Wage
A Weaton	40	250	£400.00	£0.00	£400.00
J Davis	40	295	£400.00	£7.50	£407.50
M Laston	40	280	£400.00	£0.00	£400.00

Task 7

(a)

	A	B	C	D	E	F	G
1	Month	Variable Materials £	Variable Labour £	Fixed Costs £	Total Costs £	Sales Revenue £	Profit £
2	Jan	70,000	30,000	40,000	140,000	200,000	60,000
3	Feb	140,000	60,000	40,000	240,000	400,000	160,000
4	March	105,000	45,000	40,000	190,000	300,000	110,000
5	Total	=B2+B3+B4	=C2+C3+C4	=D2+D3+D4	=E2+E3+E4	=F2+F3+F4	=G2+G3+G4

Note – other valid formulas could be used, for example using 'SUM' formulas.

(b)

	A	B	C	D	E
1		Budget £	Actual £	Variance £	A / F
2	Income	290,000	296,000	=C2-B2	F
3	Materials	144,500	150,600	=B3-C3	A
4	Labour	51,100	49,000	=B4-C4	F
5	Overheads	72,500	76,300	=B5-C5	A
6	Profit	=B2-B3-B4-B5	=C2-C3-C4-C5	=C6-B6	A

Note – other valid formulas could be used.

Answers to practice assessment 2

Task 1

(a)

Characteristic	Financial Accounting	Management Accounting
The system is subject to many external regulations	✓	
The accounts must be produced in a format that is imposed on the organisation	✓	
The system is governed primarily by its usefulness to its internal users		✓
The information produced can be in any format that the organisation wishes to use		✓

(b)

Cost	Materials	Labour	Overheads
Wood used in garden chairs	✓		
Rent of factory			✓
Wages of carpenters in the joinery section		✓	
Expenses of the office manager			✓

Task 2

(a)

	Machine hour	**Labour hour**	**Unit**
Overheads £	380,000	380,000	380,000
Activity	20,000	35,000	75,000
Absorption rate £	19.00	10.86	5.07

(b)

Cost	Machine hour £	Labour hour £	Unit £
Material	30.00	30.00	30.00
Labour	4.00	4.00	4.00
Direct cost	34.00	34.00	34.00
Overheads	3.17	2.72	5.07
Total unit cost	37.17	36.72	39.07

(c) **(1)** Where an organisation produces many different products with different values it **should not** use a per unit overhead absorption method.

(2) For a labour-intensive manufacturing organisation, the most appropriate overhead absorption method would be **direct labour hours**.

Task 3

(a)

Transaction	Code
Revenue from project in Saudi Arabia	PR200
Cost of material used for project in Saudi Arabia	PC030
Cost of hiring local labour for project in Saudi Arabia	PC040
Investment in project in Saudi Arabia	IP200
Revenue from UK project	PR100
Cost of renting project offices	PC050

(b)

Term	
Materials	✓
Fixed	
Administration	
Indirect	
Labour	✓

Task 4

	5,000 units	6,000 units	10,000 units	10,500 units
Variable cost £	17,500	21,000	35,000	36,750
Fixed cost £	1,500	1,500	1,500	1,500
Total cost £	19,000	22,500	36,500	38,250
Unit cost £	3.80	3.75	3.65	3.64

Task 5

	£		£
Closing inventory of raw materials	10,000	Opening inventory of raw materials	9,000
Direct labour	86,000	Purchases of raw materials	48,000
Opening inventory of raw materials	9,000	Closing inventory of raw materials	10,000
Closing inventory of finished goods	25,000	Direct materials used	47,000
Direct cost		Direct labour	86,000
Cost of goods manufactured	195,000	Direct cost	**133,000**
Cost of goods sold		Manufacturing overheads	64,000
Manufacturing cost	197,000	Manufacturing cost	197,000
Purchases of raw materials	48,000	Opening inventory of work in progress	9,000
Opening inventory of work in progress	9,000	Closing inventory of work in progress	11,000
Opening inventory of finished goods	30,000	Cost of goods manufactured	195,000
Manufacturing overheads	64,000	Opening inventory of finished goods	30,000
Direct materials used	47,000	Closing inventory of finished goods	25,000
Closing inventory of work in progress	11,000	Cost of goods sold	**200,000**

Task 6

(a)

Method	Cost of Issue on 18 February	Value of Inventory at 28 February
FIFO	£3,420	£3,030
LIFO	£3,480	£2,970
AVCO	£3,440	£3,010

(b)

	Hours	Cost £
Basic hours and pay	1,400	14,000
Unsocial hours premium		1,400
Overtime hours basic rate	200	2,000
Overtime hours premium		500
Bonus payment		1,600
Total pay		19,500

Task 7

Note – in this solution, the figures are provided in addition to the formulas to assist with understanding.

	A	B	C	D	E	F
1	Budgeted sales units		13,000	Budgeted selling price per unit £		64
2	Budgeted material kg		14,150	Budgeted material price per kg £		11
3	Budgeted labour hours		14,130	Budgeted labour rate per hour £		19
4	Budgeted overheads £		189,500			
5						
6		Budget £	Actual £	Variance £	Adv / Fav	Variance %
7	Sales	832,000 =C1*F1	824,000	-8,000 =C7-B7	A	-0.96 =D7/B7*100
8	Material	155,650 =C2*F2	149,960	5,690 =B8-C8	F	3.66 =D8/B8*100
9	Labour	268,470 =C3*F3	281,050	-12,580 =B9-C9	A	-4.69 =D9/B9*100
10	Overheads	189,500 =C4	191,400	-1,900 =B10-C10	A	-1.00 =D10/B10*100
11	Profit	218,380 =B7-B8-B9-B10	201,590	-16,790 =C11-B11	A	-7.69 =D11/B11*100

If the percentage function is used to calculate the percentages, then the multiplication by 100 will not be required in the formulas.

Answers to practice assessment 3

Task 1

(a)

Characteristic	Financial Accounting	Management Accounting
One of its main outputs is a summarised historical financial statement that is produced annually	✓	
One of its main purposes is useful information about costs within the organisation		✓
It can involve making comparisons between actual costs and budgeted costs		✓
Its output is controlled by legislation and accounting standards	✓	

(b)

Cost	Materials	Labour	Overheads
Aluminium used for window frames	✓		
Insurance of factory			✓
Glass used to make windows	✓		
Pay of employee who cuts glass to size and fits it into frames		✓	

Task 2

(a)

	Machine hour	**Labour hour**	**Unit**
Overheads £	1,200,000	1,200,000	1,200,000
Activity	90,000	235,000	255,000
Absorption rate £	13.33	5.11	4.71

(b)

Cost	**Machine hour £**	**Labour hour £**	**Unit £**
Material	337.50	337.50	337.50
Labour	23.00	23.00	23.00
Direct cost	360.50	360.50	360.50
Overheads	6.67	5.11	4.71
Total unit cost	367.17	365.61	365.21

Task 3

(a)

	Cost centre	**Profit centre**	**Investment centre**
An autonomous overseas division of a multi-national organisation			✓
An assembly section within a factory production department	✓		
The electrical goods section within a department store		✓	

(b)

Transaction	Code
Revenue from sale of Ford car to Mr Smith	W/300
Cost of maintenance of electronic diagnostic equipment used for servicing vehicles	Y/200
Revenue from servicing vehicles during April	W/400
Purchase cost of second hand cars at auction	X/100
Cost of oil used to service vehicles	Y/100
Cost of wax used to polish cars ready for sale	X/200

Task 4

	12,000 units	12,500 units	16,000 units	16,500 units
Variable cost £	216,000	225,000	288,000	297,000
Fixed cost £	63,400	63,400	63,400	63,400
Total cost £	279,400	288,400	351,400	360,400
Cost per unit £	23.28	23.07	21.96	21.84

Task 5

(a)

Cost structure for last period	£
Prime cost	293,000
Manufacturing overheads	126,000
Total manufacturing cost	419,000
Cost of goods manufactured	407,000
Cost of goods sold	424,000

(b)   **Text wrapping** involves automatically using additional lines within a cell so that longer text can be seen.

Merging involves joining two adjacent cells together.

Borders can be used to place thick lines around the outside of a selected cell or group of cells.

Task 6

(a)

	Receipts			Issues			Balance	
Date	Qty (kg)	Cost per kg	Total cost £	Qty (kg)	Cost per kg	Total cost £	Qty (kg)	Total cost £
1 Dec							20,000	50,000
6 Dec	15,000	2.65	39,750				35,000	89,750
9 Dec				20,000	2.6125	52,250	15,000	37,500

(b)

Method	Valuation of Issue £	Closing inventory value £
FIFO	50,000	39,750
AVCO	51,286	38,464

(c)

Worker	Hours Worked	Units Produced	Basic Wage	Bonus	Gross Wage
J Jarvis	40	150	£440.00	£0.00	£440.00
S Poole	40	185	£440.00	£37.50	£477.50
D Kerr	40	173	£440.00	£19.50	£459.50

Task 7

Note – in this solution, the figures are provided in addition to the formulas to assist with understanding.

	A	B	C	D	E	F
1	Budgeted sales units for month	10,500	Budgeted selling price per unit £	12		
2	Budgeted material for month kg	15,600	Budgeted material price per kg £	1.50		
3	Budgeted labour hours for month	1,060	Budgeted labour rate per hour £	18		
4	Budgeted annual overheads £	720,000				
5						
6		Budget £	Actual £	Variance £	Adv / Fav	Variance %
7	Sales	126,000 =C1*F1	120,500	-5,500 =C7-B7	A	-4.37 =D7/B7*100
8	Material	23,400 =C2*F2	25,000	-1600 =B8-C8	A	-6.84 =D8/B8*100
9	Labour	19,080 =C3*F3	19,500	-420 =B9-C9	A	-2.20 =D9/B9*100
10	Overheads	60,000 =C4/12	61,000	-1,000 =B10-C10	A	-1.67 =D10/B10*100
11	Profit	23,520 =B7-B8-B9-B10	15,000	-8,520 =C11-B11	A	-36.22 =D11/B11*100

If the percentage function is used to calculate the percentages, then the multiplication by 100 will not be required in the formulas.

The formula for cell B11 could alternatively be: =B7-SUM(B8:B10)

for your notes

for your notes